Football

RULES OF THE GAME

Jim Kelman

HODDER
Wayland

an imprint of Hodder Children's Books

Other titles in the series:
Skills of the Game
Players and Tactics
Teamwork!

For more information on this series
and other Hodder Wayland titles,
go to www.hodderwayland.co.uk

Produced for Wayland
Publishers Limited by
Thunderbolt Partnership
Editors: Paula Field
Janet de Saulles
Designer: Eljay Yidirim
Photography: Steve Gorton
Artwork: Phillp Morrision

First published by
Wayland Publishers Limited
This edition published in 2006
by Hodder Wayland, an imprint
of Hodder Children's Books
338 Euston Road, London NW1 3BH

© Copyright 1999 Hodder Wayland

British Library Cataloguing
in Publication Data
Kelman, Jim
Knowing the Rules. - (Soccer)
1. Soccer - Juvenile literature
1.Title 796 . 3' 34
ISBN-10: 0750249447
ISBN-13: 9780750249447

Printed in China

Foreword from Sir Clive Woodward:

For all young children who take part in the game of football, these books will give an excellent insight into the techniques and understanding that will help them to become more knowledgeable and improve their playing skills.

Contents

Introduction

Football is the most popular game in the world. It can be played anywhere, from small, remote villages in Africa and the beaches of Brazil to the packed grounds of the world's greatest football stadiums.

Anyone can play

Football is a game for people of all ages and abilities, not just the young and fit. Throughout the world thousands of people with learning disabilities regularly take part. Football is played by the blind, and has been included in the Deaf World Games. There is also a World Championship for amputees.

▶These boys are playing football on a bit of grassy ground. You don't need teams or kit to start playing footie!

4

▲ These Kenyan
schoolgirls have even
made their own ball.

◀ The loud roar of the
supporters makes a
football match really
exciting, both for the
players and the crowd.

In this book you will learn about mini-
soccer and eleven a-side, the best-
known type of football. You'll also get
some ideas about football-based games
you can play that will help when you
play a full match.

Getting started

PLAYING ALONE

To play football, all you need is yourself and a ball. The simplest games develop ball skills. You can easily practise these by yourself.

Getting a feel for the ball

Try touching the ball with different parts of your feet. The inside, the outside, the top, the bottom and your heel can be used to move the ball in different directions.

PRACTICE MAKES PERFECT

▶ Use different parts of both of your feet to move the ball around.

Keep-ups

Next, try to keep the ball in the air with different parts of your body. Use your feet, thighs, chest and head.

▶ Practise keep-ups by passing the ball from your head to first one thigh, then the other, then from foot to foot. Now start all over again without the ball touching the ground.

◀ Heading the ball or shooting against a wall is great fun, especially if there is a target to aim for.

▶ Improve your ball control by balancing the ball in as many different ways as possible.

PLAYING WITH OTHERS

Whenever you have some spare time, you can play football with your friends or family.

▼ Pass the ball to your friends in as many ways as possible.

Getting better at football

Playing football with a group of friends is much more exciting than practising ball skills alone, because you can pass the ball to each other. You can make the ball go along the ground or in the air using different parts of your feet and your body.

SWERVE THE PASS BY SPINNING THE BALL AS YOU KICK IT

A balanced position

To play passing or keep-up games you must get into a balanced position and be quick to decide which part of your body you are going to use next.

▲ Head the ball from friend to friend without letting the ball touch the floor.

▼ Try playing shooting games with one player in goal and the other players trying to score.

Using your skills

Players who are trying to score can practice using their ball skills to keep the ball away from the opposition before shooting for goal.

▶ Challenging other players for the ball is an important part of playing football.

Playing in a team

PLAYING MINI-SOCCER

Many young people aged between 5 and 11 years old often learn how to play football by playing mini-soccer. You should have between three and seven players on each side, but the older the players the more team members you can have.

Length of play

A mini-soccer game can last as long as you like, depending on the age of the players.

How to play

The object of the game is to move the ball into the other team's half of the pitch. Then you score by kicking or heading the ball into their goal.

▲ You will probably feel tired after a game of mini-soccer because you have been running around and having fun. But if you play regularly, you will get fitter and feel less tired.

Some laws

Mini-soccer is very easy to play, but there are laws that you must learn. Here are some of them:

⚽ You and your team can use all of the pitch.

⚽ You play as both an attacker and a defender.

⚽ Substitutes can go on and come off at any time.

⚽ If one of the teams has less players, the goalkeeper can come out on to the pitch and help his team mates.

▲ You do not need a lot of space to play mini-soccer – your school playground would be ideal.

COACH'S NOTES

Try to let all players, including the substitutes, on the pitch for the same amount of time.

Mini-soccer has a game leader rather than a referee. The game leader is not allowed on the playing area.

MORE ABOUT MINI-SOCCER

What you wear when playing mini-soccer depends upon the time of year. It also varies according to the surface you are playing on.

◀ Your football shoes should have a good grip. This really helps on slippery pitches.

All weathers

If it is cold, wet and muddy, wrap up well in a tracksuit or layers of warm clothing. But if the weather is hot, take off some of the layers, play in training shoes and enjoy the sunshine.

▲ The mini-soccer pitch can be inside or outside, but most pitches are outdoors, in parks and school playgrounds.

The pitch

The size of pitch should suit the age and the size of whoever is playing the game, getting bigger as the players get older. It is marked out with lines or plastic markers.

The goal posts should be 2m x 3m.

MAXIMUM

The penalty area is across the full length of the pitch.
The goal kick can be taken anywhere along the edge of the penalty area.

55m

20m

For games between players aged 10 and 11 years old, the pitch should be 55m x 39m.

MINIMUM

30m

For games between players aged 6 and 7 years old the pitch should be 30m x 20m.

39m

▲ The maximum and minimum sizes of a mini football pitch.

13

PLAYING ELEVEN A-SIDE

By practising football through playing mini-soccer, you will soon be ready to play eleven a-side. This is played by two teams of eleven players. The match can last for 90 minutes, and in the middle there is a ten-minute break.

◀ An eleven a-side pitch must be between 90m and 120m long and between 45m and 90m wide.

Joining a club

Club football is played all over the world. Boys and girls usually start playing in their own teams from around 12 years old. Your local club will be able to tell you how good you are, which position you are most suited for and which of their teams you could play in.

A team game

To begin with, the most important thing is to enjoy playing. But playing eleven a-side depends on teamwork. This means trying always to know where your team mates are, and helping them.

ENCOURAGE WHEN THINGS GO WRONG AND GIVE PRAISE WHEN THINGS GO WELL.

COACH'S NOTES

Football is a team game, Good 'team players' always help each other out during the game.

▲ A good-size crowd watches as the action hots up in the second half of this senior non-league match. Smaller club matches can draw loyal supporters even on a cold winter's day.

FOOTBALL KITS

When you are part of
a team you will play
in its colours.

The away kit

If you play against
a team which has
the same colours
as your own, then one
of the teams changes its kit.
This is called an away kit,
as it is usually the away
team that has to change.

A footballer's kit includes
shirts, shorts, socks, shin
pads and boots.

▼ The shirts worn in league
football are numbered.

▼ League teams
usually have a logo
which is often on
the front of the shirt.

◀ Always wear shin pads.
These can be just simple shin
bone protectors or they might have
built-in ankle protectors.

The goalkeeper
Goalkeepers wear a kit which is a different colour from both their own team's kit and the opposition's.

Gloves
The goalkeeper's gloves must not be too loose. They will help to grip the ball when it is wet.

Boots
Your boots are probably the most important part of your kit. There are many types of boots available and the type you buy depends on what sort of football you play and where you play it.

◀ Some football boots have a moulded sole for playing on dry summer surfaces. Others have screw-in studs which can be changed in the summer and winter.

▲ For playing indoors or on astro turf you can wear special training shoes.

The ref decides...

Both mini-soccer and eleven a-side football play with two teams on the pitch, but in eleven-a-side, there is another team – the referee and assistant referees.

Fair play

The referee is on the pitch to make sure that you play safely and fairly. He or she is also a timekeeper, noting all the times for stoppages and blowing the final whistle after 90 minutes of football has been played. The referee and assistant referees usually wear black, so they can be identified easily.

▲ The referee blows a whistle and uses special arm movements to tell the players what he has decided.

▼ The referee signals for an indirect free kick in this local league friendly.

THE
REFEREE'S
DECISION IS
FINAL!

Stopping and starting

The referee blows a whistle to stop and start play. The assistant referees wave a flag when the ball is out of play or when a player breaks the laws.

▲ A referee usually runs diagonally across the pitch, keeping up with the play. His assistants run up and down their half of the touch line, level with the attack – this system means that all areas of the pitch are covered.

FOULS AND FREE KICKS

When a player breaks a law of the game, the referee may award the other team a free kick, an indirect free kick or a penalty. The player breaking the laws may be given a warning, or even sent off.

Direct free kick

For certain offences (see page 28/29), the referee awards a free kick. This means that the person taking the free kick can kick the ball without being challenged by the opposition players. You can score straight from a direct free kick.

▲ If the offence takes place inside the penalty area, the referee will award a penalty. When a penalty is taken, the goalkeeper is not allowed to move off his line until the ball is kicked.

Indirect free kick

For some offences (see page 28/29), the referee will award an indirect free kick. You cannot score a goal straight from an indirect free kick. The ball has to touch another player first.

Yellow cards

When a player breaks a law, the referee may warn or caution him or her by showing a yellow card. The referee will also write the player's name in a book.

Red cards

If a player is guilty of serious foul play, such as violence against another player, the referee will show the red card and send the player off. A player who receives two yellow cards in the same match will also be sent off.

▲ If you are awarded an indirect free kick inside the opposition's goal area, the kick must be taken from the edge of the goal area. The player on the right will pass the ball to his team mate, who will try to score.

RESTARTING PLAY

Sometimes the referee stops the game because the ball has gone out of play. The game must be restarted and the referee can do this in several ways:

▼ A goal cannot be scored directly from a throw-in.

The throw-in

When the whole of the ball crosses the touchline, the referee will award a throw-in to the team that did not kick the ball out. The thrower must have part of each foot either on the touchline or on the ground outside the touchline, face the field of play and use both hands.

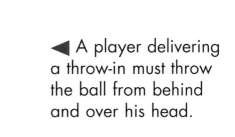

◄ A player delivering a throw-in must throw the ball from behind and over his head.

The corner kick

If a defending player kicks the ball over his own goal line but not between the posts, a corner kick is awarded to the other team. A goal may be scored directly from a corner kick.

▲ A corner kick is taken from inside the corner arc at the nearest corner flagpost, by a player of the attacking team.

The goal kick

When the ball passes over the goal line but not between the posts, and the last person to have touched the ball is a member of the attacking team, then a goal kick is awarded to the defending team.

◄ The goal kick is taken by a player of the defending team from inside the goal area. A goal can be scored directly from a goal kick.

Joining a club

Once you become good at football, you may want to join a team or club. Football clubs usually have teams for both boys and girls. Ask an adult to help you find one. The Football Association has lists of clubs in all areas.

▲ Most major football clubs have junior teams and they will run a variety of coaching sessions

Training nights

The club you join may have pre-season training nights. Also, there might be trials to find out the best players.

Signing for a club

From club trials the better players are soon spotted, and usually your parents will be contacted. This might mean that the football club wants you to sign for them.

Avoiding injuries

If you play too much eleven a-side, you may strain certain parts of your body. So stick to the number of games that your club recommends for you.

◀ If you are taken on by one of the clubs you will have to work very hard and will not spend all your time playing football.

PUSH YOURSELF – YOU MIGHT BECOME A STAR!

The big match

Many young foot-ballers dream of playing professional football but very few actually make it to the top. However, if you have that extra ability, you might be invited to attend one of the coaching sessions run by professional clubs.

Professional clubs employ talent scouts to find young players who are especially promising.

◀ In professional football, every game is a big match. Careers can be made or broken with one bad game, so every player will do his very best.

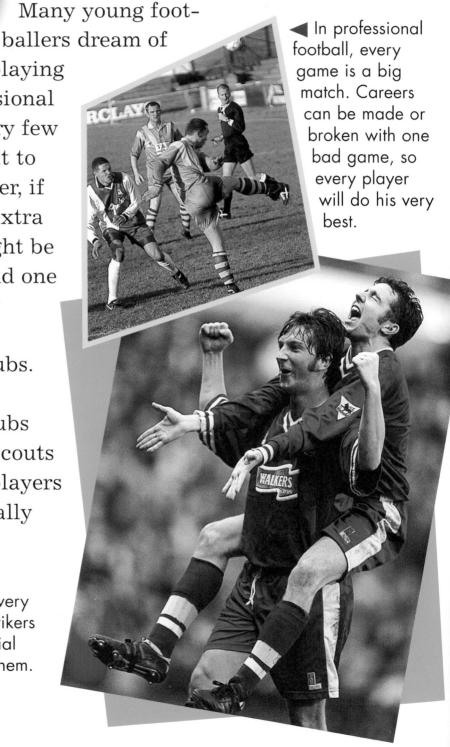

► Scoring goals is very exciting and most strikers have their own special way of celebrating them.

Football leagues

Players in the professional leagues have only one job – football! In these leagues, teams play everyone clse in their league. At the end of the season, whover has most points wins the league.

Cup competitions

Cup competitions are usually knockouts. In these, one team plays another. The winners go through to play other winners, until only two teams are left. They play the Cup Final.

▲ Great strikers will always be heavily marked by the opposition defenders, but can still score spectacular goals for their team.

LAWS OF THE GAME

There are many laws in Association Football eleven a-side football, some of which are explained below. A complete list of rules is available from the F. A.

Direct free kicks

The referee will award a direct free kick or a penalty if a player:

- kicks, trips, strikes, jumps on, pushes or charges at an opponent;
- makes contact with an opponent before touching the ball;
- holds an opponent;
- spits at an opponent;
- handles the ball (except for the goalkeeper in his or her own penalty area);
- challenges a player from behind;

He may also send off the guilty player.

▲ The referee uses his hand and arm to indicate the direction of a direct free kick.

Indirect free kicks

The referee will award an indirect free kick if a player:

- stops the progress of an opponent;
- plays in a dangerous manner;
- stops the goalkeeper releasing the ball.

▲ The referee indicates an indirect free kick. He will keep his arm raised until the ball has been played.

Offside

An indirect free kick may also be awarded if a player is offside:

You are offside if you are in your opponent's half of the pitch and there are less than two opposition players between you and the goal at the time the ball was last played.

▲ Player 1 is offside because he is in front of his team mate 2 and nearer to the goal than his two opponents as 2 is passing the ball to him.

⚽ An eleven-a-side match begins with a kick-off in the centre circle. There is a kick-off after half-time and every time a goal is scored.

⚽ Up to three substitutes may be used in any game played under National Football Association rules, or six in other games.

⚽ If a player is sent off, he cannot be replaced by a substitute. The team has to continue the match with less players.

Glossary

Amputee A person who has had a limb, or part of a limb, cut off because of an injury or a disease.

Association Football The name given to eleven-a-side football.

Attacker The player of the attacking team with the ball.

Caution When the referee shows a player the yellow card.

Club coaching Training given by a football club.

Corner kick A way of restarting the game. It is a direct free kick which is taken from the corner circle. A goal can be scored directly from a corner kick.

Cup final The final game played after a series of games where teams have played against each other on a knockout basis.

Direct free kick A type of free kick from which a goal can be scored.

Free kick A kick given to a team if a member of the the opposition commits an offence.

Goalkeeper The player who protects his or her team's goal, and who is allowed to handle the ball in the goal area.

Goal kick A kick from the goal area, which must clear the penalty area before it is in play. A goal can be scored directly from a goal kick.

Indirect free kick A type of free kick from which a goal cannot be scored.

Kick-off When the ball is put in the middle of the centre circle and kicked to restart the game. There is a kick-off at the start of a match, after half-time and every time a goal is scored.

Kit The clothes which a footballer needs to wear.

Knockout A competition in which the losing team in each match does not play again.

League football A group of football clubs which compete against each other for a prize.

Offside You are offside if you are in your opponent's half of the pitch and there are less than two opposition players between you and the goal at the time the ball was last played.

Penalty area This is the area around the goal. If a serious foul happens here, the referee will give a penalty kick.

Professional A person who plays football for money.

Red card If a player has committed a serious offence, the referee holds up the red card and sends the player off the pitch.

Substitute A player who takes over from a tired or injured player.

Throw-in A way of restarting the game after the ball has gone out of play. A goal cannot be scored directly from a throw-in.

Touchline The line that marks the edge of the pitch.

Yellow card If a player has committed a foul, the referee shows the yellow card. If a player receives two yellow cards in one match, he or she will be sent off.

Further information

Football Associations

English F.A., 25 Soho Square, London W1D 4FA
www.thefa.com

Scottish F.A., Hampden Park, Glasgow G42 9AY
www.scottishfa.co.uk

F.A. of Wales, Plymouth Chambers, 3 Westgate Street, Cardiff CF10 1DP
www.fawtrust.org.uk

Irish F.A. (Northern Ireland), 20 Windsor Avenue, Belfast BT9 6EG
www.irishfa.com

F.A. of Ireland (Republic of Ireland), 80 Merreon Square, Dubin 2
www.fai.ie

Books

Defensive Soccer Tactics by Jens Bangbo and Berger Pietersen
(Human Kinetics Europe, 2001)
SAQ Soccer: Speed, Agility and Quickness for Soccer
by Alan Pearson (A&C Black, 2001)
The Football Association Coaching Book of Soccer Tactics and Skills by
Charles Hughes (Queen Anne Press, 1994)
The Practices and Training Sessions of the World's Top Teams and Coaches
by Mike Saif (Reedswain Incorporated, 2000)
Youth Soccer Drills by Jim Garland (Human Kinetics Europe, 2003)

WEBSITE DISCLAIMER:
The website addresses (URLs) included in this book were valid at the
time of going to press. However, because of the nature of the Internet,
it is possible that some addresses may have changed, or sites may have
changed or closed down since publication. While the authors and Publisher
regret any inconvenience this may cause readers, no responsibility for any
such changes can be accepted by either the authors or the Publisher.

ACKNOWLEDGEMENTS:
We would like to thank the following people for their help
with this book:
The Football Association, Nikki Kelman, Ray Coventry and
Arsenal F.C. Soccer School, Mike Fowles and the boys and
girls of Wynchcombe Junior School, David Pembroke and
Chesham F.C., Hendon F.C., Gordon Bartlett, SCOPE.

PICTURE CREDITS:
PP 4-5 Allsport, P.12b.Colorsport, P26-27 b. Allsport, P15
Martin Wray, P.19 Garry Letts; Tony Williams Publications.

Index